PET CARE FOR KIDS

FISH

BY KATHRYN STEVENS

The Child's World

Published in the United States of America by The Child's World®
1980 Lookout Drive • Mankato, MN 56003-1705
800-599-READ • www.childsworld.com

Acknowledgments
The Child's World®: Mary Berendes, Publishing Director
The Design Lab: Kathleen Petelinsek, Design and Page Production

Photo Credits: Cherie Moncada/dreamstime.com: 13; Chode/
dreamstime.com: front cover, 1, 8 (stones); Dohnal/dreamstime.
com: front cover (danio); Donkeyru/dreamstime.com: 7; Frans Sluijs/
dreamstime.com: front cover, 3, 22 (platy); Halilo/dreamstime.com:
10 (filter); Ian Scott/dreamstime.com: front cover, back cover, 1, 3,
4, 22 (blue tang); iStockphoto.com/Eric Isselée: front cover, 1, 21,
22 (clownfish); iStockphoto.com/Kristen Johansen: front cover, 8,
22 (plant); iStockphoto.com/Lars Christensen: front cover, 1, 3 (net);
iStockphoto.com/Ralf Hirsch: 17; iStockphoto.com/Scott Hirko:
5; iStockphoto.com/Tatjana Rittner: front cover, back cover, 1, 3,
4, 24 (yellow tang); Kateryna Dyellalova/dreamstime.com: back
cover, 20 (supplies); Kathleen Petelinsek: back cover, 3, 14, 20 (food);
M_agullo/dreamstime.com: 9; Marcelo Saavedra/dreamstime.com:
front cover, 1 (plecostomus); Paul Hardy/Corbis: 19; Petar Lazovic/
dreamstime.com: 11; Peter Pomorski/dreamstime.com: 15; Podius/
dreamstime.com:16, 20; Serdar Yagci/iStockphoto.com: 6

Library of Congress Cataloging-in-Publication Data
Stevens, Kathryn, 1954–
  Fish / by Kathryn Stevens.
    p. cm. — (Pet care for kids)
  Includes index.
  ISBN 978-1-60253-182-6 (library bound : alk. paper)
  1. Aquarium fishes—Juvenile literature. 2. Aquariums—Juvenile
literature. I. Title. II. Series.
  SF457.25.S88 2009
  639.34—dc22   2008040109

NOTE TO PARENTS AND EDUCATORS

The Pet Care for Kids series is written for children who want to be part of the pet experience but are too young to be in charge of pets themselves. These books are intended to provide a kid-friendly supplement to more detailed information adults need to know about choosing and caring for different types of pets. They can help youngsters learn how to live happily with the animals in their lives, and, with adults' help and supervision, grow into responsible animal caretakers later on.

CONTENTS

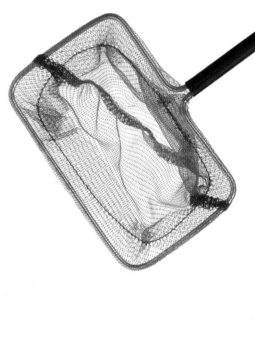

FISH AS PETS

Fish make interesting pets! People love to see them up close. They enjoy their bright, flashing colors. Even little babies like to watch fish swim. Some kinds of fish are easy to keep as pets. Others take special care.

▶ This tank is full of Malawi cichlids (SIH-kledz).

▼ Tangs are fish that live in salty water. There are many different types. This blue tang and yellow tang look very different!

Some kinds of fish live together well. Others do not. They might fight or even eat each other. Size is something to think about, too. Many fish start out small but keep getting bigger. They need a big enough place to live.

▶ People often keep goldfish as pets. But many goldfish can grow too big for small fish tanks.

◀ Betta (BAY-tuh) fish like this one are also called Siamese fighting fish. Male bettas cannot be kept together, or they will fight.

A NICE HOME

Pet fish live in clear tanks called **aquariums**. The fish should have plenty of room to swim. They like places to hide, too. Rocks make great hiding places. So do underwater plants. **Gravel** covers the bottom of the aquarium. It comes in different colors.

▶ This aquarium has lots of hiding places for fish.

▼ Some aquarium plants are real. Others are made of plastic.

CLEAN WATER

Fish spend their whole lives underwater. They even breathe underwater. Air bubbling through the water helps them breathe. A **filter** helps keep the water clean. Sometimes aquariums need more careful cleaning.

▶ A bubbler puts air into the tank for these cichlids.

◀ People with pet fish learn how to keep the aquarium clean.

Some pet fish live in saltwater. It is salty like the sea. But most pet fish live in freshwater. It is not salty. Some fish need cold water. Others need warmer water. Water from the tap can make fish ill. Special pills or drops make it safer. So does letting it sit for a few days.

This aquarium has saltwater fish. The big, striped ones are Moorish idol fish. You can also see a blue tang, a yellow tang, and some smaller fish.

Pet stores sell special drops for fish tanks. It makes the water safer for fish.

GOOD FOOD

Pet fish eat special fish foods. Different fish eat different kinds of food. Feeding fish is easy. You just sprinkle the food on top of the water. They only need a little at a time. Too much food makes the water dirty.

This goldfish is eating food flakes that are floating on top of the water.

Fish food often comes in thin flakes.

GOOD HEALTH

Some pet fish live for only two or three years. Others can live for 20! Taking good care of them helps. Careful feeding is important. So is keeping the aquarium clean. Sometimes fish get sick anyway. Animal doctors, or **vets**, can often help. So can pet stores.

▶ Plecos (PLEE-kohz) are great to have in a fish tank. They eat gunk that grows on the glass. They are a fun way to keep the tank clean!

◀ A cover keeps the fish from jumping out of the tank. It keeps cats away, too!

LOVING CARE

Fish are not cuddly like some pets. But they are fun to watch! A nice, clean aquarium is bright and beautiful. The fish in it will stay healthy. And people will enjoy seeing them swim in their underwater world.

▶ This aquarium is clean and bright. Watching its colorful fish is lots of fun!

NEEDS:

* the right-sized aquarium
* a water filter
* bubbling air
* hiding places
* the right food
* aquarium cleaning

DANGERS:

* no aquarium top
* dirty water
* no air in the water
* too much food
* soap or cleaners
* heat or cold
* too much sunlight
* the wrong fish living together

SCALES:
A fish's body is covered with thin scales.

BODIES:
Fishes' body shapes move easily through the water.

EYES:
Fish do not have eyelids. They never close their eyes, even when they sleep.

SIZE:
Some goldfish grow to be 1 foot (30 centimeters) long!

GILLS:
Fish breathe by moving water through their gills.

FINS:
Fish use their fins to move and steer in the water.

GLOSSARY

aquariums (*uh-KWAYR-ee-ums*) Aquariums are clear tanks where animals can live.

filter (*FIL-tur*) A fish-tank filter cleans dirt and food out of the water.

gravel (*GRA-vul*) Gravel for fish tanks is made up of small, round stones.

vets (*VETS*) Vets are doctors who take care of animals. Vet is short for "veterinarian" (*vet-rih-NAYR-ee-un*).

TO FIND OUT MORE

Books:

Algarra, Alejandro, Rosa Maria Curto (illustrator), and Sally-Ann Hopwood (translator). *Our New Fish*. New York: Barron's Educational Series, 2008.

Evans, Mark. *Fish*. New York: Dorling Kindersley, 2001.

Morley, Christine, Carole Orbell, and Brita Granström (illustrator). *Me and My Pet Fish*. Chicago, IL: World Book Encyclopedia, 1997.

Video/DVD:

Paws, Claws, Feathers & Fins: A Kid's Guide to Happy, Healthy Pets. Goldhil Learning Series (Video 1993, DVD 2005).

Web Sites:

Visit our Web page for lots of links about pet care:
http://www.childsworld.com/links

Note to parents, teachers, and librarians: We routinely verify our Web links to make sure they are safe, active sites—so encourage your readers to check them out!

INDEX

ABOUT THE AUTHOR

Kathryn Stevens has authored and edited many books for young readers, including books on animals ranging from grizzly bears to fleas. She's a lifelong pet-lover and currently cares for a big, huggable pet-therapy dog named Fudge.